FROM FERGUSON TO FRANKFURT

From Ferguson to Frankfurt

Examining Police Use of Deadly Force in the United States and Germany

Michael A. Caves

INTRODUCTION

In early August of 2014, news outlets from all of the country began reporting on the death of Michael Brown, an 18 year old African-American man who was unarmed when he was shot and killed by a white police officer in Ferguson, Missouri (Chuck, 2014; Brown, 2014). In the weeks and months immediately following Brown's death, details of the shooting began to emerge, as violence erupted on the streets of Ferguson (Brown, 2014). Within twelve hours of the shooting, the St. Louis County Police Chief held a press conference and confirmed that Michael Brown was unarmed when he physically assaulted the officer, who fired several shots at Brown in response (Brown, 2014). Later that night, more than a dozen local businesses were looted and vandalized, and more than 30 people were arrested (Brown, 2014).

Within days of Brown's death, President Obama addressed the nation and urged peace from protesters and transparency from local investigators (Brown, 2014). In the weeks following Brown's death, the President announced that the Attorney General would be monitoring the events in Ferguson (Brown, 2014).

Between August and late November, over 135 more people were arrested in connection with protests in Ferguson, Missouri (Brown, 2014). During the three months that followed Michael Brown's death, at least two reporters were detained by police, as civil rights leaders and reporters alike converged on Ferguson (Brown, 2014). During that same time period, the governor of Missouri declared a state of emergency, the Federal Aviation Administration instituted air restrictions over Ferguson, and National Guard units were deployed to join State highway patrol to keep the peace in Ferguson (Brown, 2014).

The death of Michael Brown dominated the news cycle for months, generating heated debate and emotional discussion all over the country on topics such as race and police authority. On November 24, 2014, when the St. Louis County grand jury announced that the police officer who fired six shots and killed Brown would not be indicted, news and video footage of the shooting of an unarmed 12 year old African-American boy by a white police officer in Cleveland was already making national headlines (Brown, 2014; Perez-Pena, 2015). By the time the U.S. Department of Justice announced in March of 2015 that the officer responsible for Michael Brown's death would not be prosecuted federally, over a dozen new, fatal officer-involved shootings had occurred throughout the U.S. (CBS News, 2015; Perez-Pena, 2015).

In light of increased media attention and public outrage in the aftermath of numerous high profile police killings in recent years, this book examines the fatal use of force by police officers in both the United States and Germany. Both nations have a history of struggling with race relations, and more recently, with immigration, both nations are industrialized, and both nations have armed law enforcement officers who are authorized to use deadly force. Similarly, both nations are federal republics, and the economies of both nations are among the largest, most productive, and innovative in the world (CIA World Factbook, 2015a; CIA World Factbook, 2015b).

Despite these similarities, the use of deadly force by law enforcement officers in Germany is exceedingly rare when compared to the rate in the United States. This book will explore the legal implications of the fatal use of force incident to arrest according to U.S. Law, German law, and international law applicable to both nations, with an eye toward revealing inconsistencies among the laws.

DEADLY FORCE BY U.S. POLICE

This section introduces the legal standards that govern deadly force by law enforcement officers in the United States, as well as the policies and standards of U.S. Police Departments for using deadly force. Rates of deadly force in the U.S. are discussed, as well as the international standards that might also be applicable to the use of deadly force in the United States. Finally, inconsistencies between relevant international law and U.S. law are explored.

U.S. LEGAL STANDARDS GOVERNING DEADLY FORCE

The three primary sources of federal legal standards that govern the use of force by officers in the United States are Title 42 United States Code § 1983, and the U.S. Supreme Court cases of *Graham v. Connor* and *Tennessee v. Garner* (Leonnig, 2014; McElvain, 2009).

Title 42, United States Code § 1983 reads as follows:

"Every person who, under color of any statute, ordinance, regulation, custom, or usage, of any State or the District of Columbia, subjects, or causes to be subjected, any citizen of the United States or other person within the jurisdiction thereof to the deprivation

of any rights, privileges, or immunities secured by the

Constitution and laws, shall be liable to the party

injured in an action at law, suit in equity, or other

proper proceeding for redress..."

(42 U.S.C. § 1983).

In 1985, the Supreme Court decided the case of

Tennessee v. Garner (471 U.S. 1). The Court held that a

Tennessee statute that permitted officers to use all

necessary force to effect an arrest was inconsistent with

the Fourth Amendment of the U.S. Constitution, as the

State statute did not contemplate the kind of analysis

required under the Fourth Amendment. Specifically, the

court found that the Fourth Amendment requires

weighing the intrusion on a protected Fourth Amendment interest against the importance of the government interest used to justify the intrusion (*Id.*).

In particular, the Court was concerned that the Tennessee statute as applied permitted the use of deadly force to effect an arrest for any offense, without any consideration of the danger posed by the fleeing suspect (*Id.*). In discussing why the use of deadly force in detaining or arresting a suspect is subject to a Fourth Amendment analysis, as opposed to some other constitutional or statutory standard, the Court in *Tennessee v. Garner* explained in relevant part as follows:

"Whenever an officer restrains the freedom of a person to walk away, he has seized that person. While it is not always clear just when minimal police interference becomes a seizure, there can be no question that apprehension by the use of deadly force is a seizure subject to the reasonableness requirement of the Fourth Amendment."

(*Tennessee v. Garner*, 1985, PAGE) (Citations omitted).

The Court described the general Fourth Amendment balancing analysis for the use of deadly force in apprehending a suspect as follows:

"To determine the constitutionality of a seizure we must balance the nature and quality of the intrusion on the individual's Fourth Amendment interests against the importance of the governmental interests alleged to justify the intrusion. We have described the balancing of competing interests as the key principle of the Fourth Amendment."

(*Tennessee v. Garner*, 1985) (Citations omitted).

Finally, the Court indicated that it could be constitutionally permissible under Fourth Amendment to use deadly force in apprehending a suspect in certain circumstances:

"Where the officer has probable cause to believe that the suspect poses a threat of serious physical harm, either to the officer or to others, it is not constitutionally

unreasonable to prevent escape by using deadly force."

(*Tennessee v. Garner*, 1985, at 23).

A few years later in 1989, the Supreme Court

issued its opinion in *Graham v. Connor* (490 U.S. 386).

Chief Justice Rehnquist, who dissented from the

Court's opinion in *Tennessee v. Garner,* delivered the

opinion of the Court (*Tennessee v. Garner*, 1985, at 12;

Graham v. Connor, 1989, at 388). After discussing the

fact that constitutional protection from physically

abusive government conduct is based on either the

Fourth Amendment or the Eighth Amendment.

With regard to whether a particular occurrence of use of force by police should be examined under the Fourth Amendment or the Eighth Amendment, the court explained that claims alleging excessive force during arrest are analyzed under the Fourth Amendment, while claims of excessive force used on convicted prisoners (who are already in police custody, where the use of force is not incident to arrest) are analyzed under the Eighth Amendment. The court reasoned that the use of force incident to arrest is a 'seizure' within the meaning of the Fourth Amendment. In contrast, use of force by officers against a prisoner who is already in custody properly falls under the 'cruel and unusual punishment' prohibition addressed by the Eighth Amendment.

The Court went on to describe the amorphous nature of the "reasonableness" test as follows:

"The test of reasonableness under the Fourth Amendment is not capable of precise definition, however, its proper application requires careful attention to the facts and circumstances of each particular case, including the severity of the crime at issue, whether the suspect poses an immediate threat to the safety of the officers or others, and whether he is actively resisting arrest or attempting to evade arrest by flight."

(*Graham v. Connor*, 1989, at 396) (Citations omitted).

Finally, the Court clarified that the "reasonableness" test is an objective one, rather than subjective, but that the analysis should consider the perspective of a reasonable officer in the same position:

"The 'reasonableness' of a particular use of force must be judged from the perspective of a reasonable officer on the scene, rather than with the 20/20 vision of hindsight...The calculus of reasonableness must embody allowance for the fact that police officers are often forced to make split-second judgments--in circumstances that are tense, uncertain, and rapidly evolving--about the amount of force that is necessary in a particular situation. As in other Forth Amendment contexts, however, the 'reasonableness' inquiry in an excessive force case is an objective one: the question is whether the officers' actions are 'objectively reasonable' in light of the facts and circumstances confronting them, without regard to their underlying intent or motivation ."

(*Graham v. Connor*, 1989, at 396) (Citations omitted).

In addition to the standards outlined in federal statutes and caselaw, many States have their own laws governing use of force by officers. California's standard for use of force is typical of State statutes on the subject.

The standard in California is codified in Penal Code section 835a, which reads as follows:

"Any peace officer who has reasonable cause to believe that the person to be arrested has committed a public offense may use reasonable force to effect the arrest, to prevent escape or to overcome resistance.

A peace officer who makes or attempts to make an arrest need not retreat or desist from his efforts by reason of the resistance or threatened resistance of the person being arrested; nor shall such officer be deemed an aggressor or lose his right to self-defense by the use of reasonable force to effect the arrest or to prevent escape or to overcome resistance."

(Cal. Pen. Code § 835a).

The language of the applicable California Penal Code is consistent with the 'reasonable force' language outlined in the Supreme Court's Fourth Amendment analysis in both *Tennessee v. Garner* and *Graham v. Connor* (McElvain, 2009). Similarly, the relevant California civil jury instruction for use of deadly force by officers is consistent with the Court's 'totality of the circumstances' test in Fourth Amendment cases.

The applicable California civil jury instruction (BAJI 3.43) reads as follows:

"In determining whether a law enforcement officer exercised reasonable care in using deadly force, you should consider the totality of the circumstances which preceded the use of deadly force, including the officer's tactical conduct and decisions before the use of force. An officer in making a decision to use deadly force is entitled to rely on circumstances as they reasonably appear to [him] [or] [her]."

(BAJI, 2014, at 3.43).

The prospect of having 50 different laws governing use of force among the various U.S. States would be unmanageable. Fortunately, since police use of force standards addressed in State statute are based on rights protected by the Fourth Amendment of the U.S. Constitution, the language of state laws governing use of force by officers should be generally consistent with the federal standards. In fact, it was State statute inconsistency with Fourth Amendment jurisprudence that led to the Court declaring the Tennessee statute invalid in *Tennessee v. Garner*.

Similarly, although there will be some variation among the States, the civil standard for a negligence suit in California (at least where the officer intentionally fires a weapon) under the laws of the state should be precluded where the suit is unsuccessful under 42 U.S.C. § 1983, since the "totality of the circumstances" test used in a § 1983 action is the same test under common law negligence for intentional shootings by law enforcement (*Hernandez v. City of Pomona*, 2009).

U.S. POLICE DEPARTMENT POLICIES ON DEADLY FORCE

In *Tennessee v. Garner*, the Supreme Court noted that as early as 1974, most large police departments had policies that allowed officers to fire weapons only when a felon presents a threat of serious bodily harm or death (*Tennessee v. Garner*, 1985, at 20). Obviously, the risk of civil liability (and perhaps even criminal liability) for officers where conduct deviates from the federal standard, would tend to lead to standardized policies at police departments throughout the United States, at least to the extent that all of the polices would be consistent with the minimum legal standards of the Court's reasonableness analysis under the totality of the circumstances. Consistent with this assumption, the vast majority of law enforcement agencies across the country have adopted some standard for the use of fatal force that is consistent with the Fourth Amendment analysis outlined in both *Tennessee v. Garne*r and *Graham v. Connor*, although significant differences do exist among the various departments as to the level of policy specificity (McElvain, 2009).

A number of nationwide organizations exist that promote and assist departments in adopting uniform use of force policies. One such organization is the Commission on Accreditation for Law Enforcement Agencies, which, as the Court in *Tennessee v. Garner* mentioned, requires departments seeking accreditation to "...restrict the use of deadly force to situations where the officer reasonably believes that the action is in defense of human life, or in the defense of any person in immediate danger of serious physical injury" (*Tennessee v. Garner*, 1985, at page 20). Another such organization is LEXIPOL, a private company that helps police departments develop use of force policies that are consistent with constitutional standards as outlined by the Supreme Court (McElvain, 2009).

Some police departments use language that mirrors the fact-dependent balancing test addressed by the Supreme Court, while other departments have sought to explicitly spell out restrictions on fatal use of force, typically by adopting a far more conservative position than the Supreme Court would necessarily require (*Id.*, see also *Tennessee v. Garner*, 1985, at page

20). One possible justification for an overly conservative approach to fatal use of force policies is that such policies make civil and criminal liability less likely for officers, while also eliminating some guess-work by replacing the highly fact-driven balancing test of the Fourth Amendment with a bright-line rule that gives officers clear, albeit inflexible rules of engagement. Some argue that this increased clarity in use of force policies reduce the chances of delayed decision-making due to confusion in the field.

Of course, it could also be argued that a fatal use of force policy that makes it more difficult for officers to justify fatal force would also make it more likely that an officer (rather than a suspect) would get injured or killed during an encounter. Also, although officers and departments alike prefer clarity in use of force policies, the Supreme Court's analysis of use of force during arrest under the Fourth Amendment seems wholly inconsistent with a bright line rule.

In short, creating a bright-line rule from the Supreme Court's 'totality of the circumstances' test will either increase the risk of civil liability for officers (where the use of force policy is overly permissive), or will increase the risk of injury or death to officers (where the use of force policy is overly restrictive).

RATES OF U.S. POLICE USE OF DEADLY FORCE

Even in a country like the United States, fatal use of force by police during the attempted arrest or apprehension of a suspect is believed to be under-reported (Burch, 2011). Even the most comprehensive, reliable data available on arrest-related deaths from the U.S. Department of Justice's Bureau of Justice Statistics is limited by factors such as variations in reporting among different jurisdictions, partial reporting, and non-responding jurisdictions (*Id.*). In fact, when the Department of Justice began collecting arrest-related death data in 2003, only two states (California and Texas) were conducting statewide tallies of deaths related to arrest (*Id.*) Three states (Georgia, Maryland, and Montana) failed to provide any arrest-related death data during the 2003-2009 reporting periods, and participation by some other states varied from year to year (*Id.*).

Another unfortunate data limitation is the fact that the statistics from the Department of Justice on arrest-related deaths do not distinguish arrest-related deaths caused by shooting from other causes, such as blunt force trauma. Despite these challenges, the data collected and reported by the Bureau of Justice Statistics can be useful in giving researchers a sense of the general scale of the problem, as well as general trends among suspects and officers involved in arrest-related deaths.

According to the Bureau of Justice Statistics, there were around 4,800 reported arrest-related deaths in the U.S. from 2003 to 2009, compared to a total of around 98 million arrests in the US during that same period (*Id.*). Around 42% of those who died incident to arrest were white, while around 32% were black, and around 20% were Hispanic (*Id.*). Around 61% of these arrest-related deaths were determined to be homicide by law enforcement, and 11% were determined to be suicide or overdose/ intoxication (*Id.*). Only about 5% of those who died during arrest were female (*Id.*).

At first blush, the fact that nearly five thousand people were killed during the arrest process by law enforcement in the United States over the course of 8 years may leave some with the impression that fatal use of force by officers in the United States is rampant and widespread, especially when compared to the number of fatalities at the hands of police in other industrialized nations. However, when we take into account the total number of arrests during that same time period (around 98 million), it turns out that only around 0.005% of arrests in the United States from 2003-2009 resulted in the death of the suspect incident to arrest.

APPLICABLE INTERNATIONAL STANDARDS THAT COULD GOVERN DEADLY FORCE IN THE U.S.

The United States is party to a number of international treaties and agreements that address topics and standards that are relevant to the fatal use of force by officers incident to arrest. The relevant portions of applicable international instruments are addressed below.

UN Convention against Torture and Other Cruel, Inhuman or Degrading Treatment or Punishment

The United States is a party to the Convention against Torture and Other Cruel, Inhuman or Degrading

Treatment or Punishment (New York, 10 December 1984), but is not a party to the Optional Protocol to the Convention against Torture and Other Cruel, Inhuman or Degrading Treatment or Punishment (New York, 18 December 2002).

The UN Convention against Torture defines torture as follows:

"For the purposes of this Convention, the term 'torture' means any act by which severe pain or suffering, whether physical or mental, is intentionally inflicted on a person for such purposes as obtaining from him or a third person information or a confession, punishing him for an act he or a third person has committed or is suspected of having committed, or intimidating or coercing him or a third person, or for any reason based on discrimination of any kind, when such pain or suffering is inflicted by or at the instigation of or with the consent or acquiescence of a public official or other person acting in an official capacity."

(Part I, Article I, UN Convention against Torture and Other Cruel, Inhuman or Degrading Treatment or Punishment, 1984).

In applying the standard outlined in the Convention to the use of fatal force by law enforcement incident to arrest, the analysis is two-fold: the first question is whether an officer's act in using fatal force incident to arrest actually inflicts 'severe pain or suffering' intentionally, and if so, the second question is whether the act was done to gain information, punish the suspect, intimidating the suspect, or for any reason based on discrimination.

As to whether the act itself (fatal use of force by law enforcement incident to arrest) meets the first prong of the test, there is an argument to be made that shooting in particular does not inflict severe pain or suffering, particularly where the death of the suspect is very quick. However, it seems unreasonable to assume that use of force that leads to death would not constitute severe pain and suffering in most cases. As to the intent prong of the analysis, the language about coercion and intimidation seems inapplicable to the use of fatal force incident to arrest in most cases, as does the desire to gain information. The coercion, intimidation, or information-gathering language might have some applicability to situations other than use of force incident to arrest, such as in the case of traditional custodial interrogations or the use of force on prisoners. However, the discrimination language, as well as the punishment language, may apply to some instances of the use of fatal force by officers incident to arrest.

Thus, the U.N. Convention could be applicable to some cases of fatal use of force, at least where it can be shown that the officer committed the act for a discriminatory purpose or to punish the suspect for an act. It is worth noting how inconsistent the analysis here is with the Supreme Court's use of force analysis; to prove torture under the U.N. Convention, we have to consider the officer's subjective intent (inflicted pain to punish or to discriminate), while the Supreme Court's Fourth Amendment analysis is concerned with what is objectively reasonable, given the circumstances of the encounter.

This difference between subjective intent and state of mind under international law, and objective state of mind under the Fourth Amendment, forms the basis of many of the inconsistencies among various national and international standards noted in this book.

International Covenant on Civil and Political Rights

The United States is a party to the International Covenant on Civil and Political Rights, but is not a party to the Optional Protocol, nor to the Second

Optional Protocol. There are a number of Articles that could apply to the use of fatal force by officers, including Article 6(1), Article 7, and Article 26.

Article 6(1) reads as follows:

"Every human being has the inherent right to life. This right shall be protected by law. No one shall be arbitrarily deprived of his life."

(Art. 6(1), International Covenant on Civil and Political Rights, 1966).

To find that an officer's use of fatal force violated Article 6(1), it would have to be shown that the suspect was arbitrarily deprived of life. Like the international standard for torture described in the previous section, Article 6(1) also requires proof of the officer's subjective intent (rather than the objective test outlined by the Supreme Court under the Fourth Amendment), in that it would have to be shown that the officer actually deprived the individual of life without reason or cause. Curiously enough, it would seem that if the officer actually had a reason for the killing, even if the reason were otherwise unlawful, the killing would not violate Article 6(1) of the International Covenant on Civil and Political Rights

Article 7 reads in relevant part as follows:

"No one shall be subjected to torture or to cruel, inhuman or degrading treatment or punishment."

(Art. 7, International Covenant on Civil and Political Rights, 1966).

The analysis under Article 7 would mirror the torture analysis under the U.N. Convention Against Torture. Whether the officer actually has the requisite intent for the act to qualify as torture under Article 7 will depend on a subjective analysis of what was actually in the officer's mind, rather than an objective analysis of what would have been in the mind of a reasonable officer in the same circumstances.

Article 26 reads in relevant part as follows:

"All persons are equal before the law and are entitled without any discrimination to the equal protection of the law. In this respect, the law shall prohibit any discrimination and guarantee to all persons equal and effective protection against discrimination on any ground such as race, colour, sex, language, religion, political or other opinion, national or social origin, property, birth, or other status."

(Art. 26, International Covenant on Civil and Political Rights, 1966).

Here, Article 26 is violated by the use of fatal force incident to arrest only where it can be shown that the officer had discriminatory intent at the time that he acted. Again, the inquiry into intent under Article 26 is the subjective intent of the officer, rather than the objective test outlined by the Supreme Court under the Fourth Amendment.

International Convention on the Elimination of all Forms of Racial Discrimination

As the name suggests, the intent of the International Convention on the Elimination of All Forms of Racial Discrimination is to 'eliminate racial discrimination throughout the world in all its forms and manifestations' (International Convention on the Elimination of all Forms of Racial Discrimination, 1965, at paragraph 4).

Article 1 (1) defines racial discrimination as "...any distinction, exclusion, restriction or preference based on race, colour, descent, or national or ethnic origin which has the purpose or effect of nullifying or impairing the recognition, enjoyment, or exercise, on an equal footing, of human rights and fundamental freedoms in the political,economic, social, cultural or any other field of public life" (Art. 1(1), International Convention on the Elimination of All Forms of Racial Discrimination, 1965).

Article 5 (b) specifically prohibits racial discrimination that interferes with "the right to security of person and protection by the State against violence or bodily harm, whether inflicted by government officials or by any individual group or institution" (Art.

5(b), International Convention on the Elimination of All Forms of Racial Discrimination, 1965).

When Article 5(b) is read in conjunction with Article 1(1), the intent and impact of the International Convention on the Elimination of all Forms of Racial Discrimination become clear: at a minimum, government officials are prohibited from using violence or inflicting bodily harm on individuals based on distinctions of race or related characteristics, where such a distinction has the purpose or effect of diminishing that person's human rights or fundamental freedoms. One of the interesting aspects of this convention is that once it is clear that the violence or bodily injury has been inflicted due to a race-based distinction, a violation of the convention occurs even if the actual purpose is not to diminish human rights or fundamental freedoms, so long as the effect actually does diminish human rights or fundamental freedoms. The 'purpose or effect' language of the convention broadens the convention's applicability to prohibit discrimination even if the actor lacks the specific intent to diminish human rights or fundamental freedoms, so long as the actual impact is present.

In the context of fatal use of force, there is no question that ending someone's life has the effect of diminishing fundamental freedoms and human rights. As with most of the international conventions that we have analyzed under the fatal use of force scenario, the real question has to do with the actual subjective intent or mindset of the officer. If the actual reason in the officer's mind for inflicting violence or death on an individual is because of their race or a related characteristic, the officer has violated the convention. Technically this is true even if a reasonable officer in the same circumstances would have still used deadly force; the objective 'totality of the circumstances' test under the Fourth Amendment simply doesn't apply here.

Non-Binding International Instruments and Declarations

In addition to the three binding treaties discussed above that might apply in some instances of fatal force by officers in the United States, there are a number of non-binding declarations and instruments that might also apply under certain conditions. Although these instruments are not binding on the United States *per se,* the standards and obligations outlined in the instruments could still have relevance and could actually be found to be enforceable, but only if those standards and obligations qualify as international customary law, or as rules of *jus cogens* (Gallagher, 2010).

A standard is customary where "...it reflects general and uniform State practice, AND that practice is accompanied by a subjective sense of legal obligation" (Gallagher, 2010, at p. 132). Absolutely uniformity among all nations is not required; it is enough that there is a consensus that a particular standard is an actual obligation that is consistent with state practice, especially in the affected nation (*Id.*). Rules of *jus cogens,* on the other hand, are said to be peremptory norms that a generally accepted in the international community, such as the prohibition on racial discrimination (*Id.*).

While the determination of whether each otherwise non-binding declaration or standard qualifies as customary law or *jus cogens* is beyond the scope of this paper, the general standards addressed in these non-binding declarations warrant consideration. The fact that a standard is contained in an international declaration or instrument of an organization that the U.S. is party to may weigh in favor of finding that the instrument is reflective of customary law, particularly where the standard is consistent with state practice. Similarly, where the rule expressed in the instrument is "...accepted and recognized by the international community of States as a whole as a norm from which no derogation is permitted," that rule is likely to be considered a rule of *jus cogens* (*Id.*).

Both the Universal Declaration of Human Rights and the American Convention on Human rights declare a right to life, and both instruments denounce racial discrimination. It is important to note that although declarations are not binding, the U.S.is a party to the U.N., and similarly, the U.S. is a signatory to the American Convention on Human Rights, even though the U.S. never actually formally ratified, accepted, or acceded to the convention (OAS, 2015). As to the denouncement of racial discrimination and the right to life, there is an argument in favor of a finding that both are either customary law at this point, or *jus cogens*. In any event, the question is probably moot, since those concepts are covered elsewhere in binding treaties.

In addition to non-binding international instruments that seek generally to protect life and eliminate racial discrimination, a number of non-binding international instruments exist that are specific to law enforcement, and may have some applicability to the fatal use of force by officers incident to arrest. The UN Code of Conduct for Law Enforcement Officials specifies in Article 3 that "law enforcement officials may use force only when strictly necessary and to the extent required for the performance of their duty"(Art.

3, UN Code of Conduct for Law Enforcement Officials, 1980).

Similarly, part 9 of the UN Basic Principles on the Use of Force and Firearms by Law Enforcement Officials reads as follows:

"...Law enforcement officials shall not use firearms against persons except in self-defence or defence of others against the imminent threat of death or serious injury, to prevent the perpetration of a particularly serious crime involving grave threat to life, to arrest a person presenting such a danger and resisting their authority, or to prevent his or her escape, and only when less extreme means are insufficient to achieve these objectives. In any event, intentional lethal use of firearms may only be made when strictly unavoidable in order to protect life."

(Part 9, UN Basic Principles on the Use of Force and Firearms by Law Enforcement Officials, 1990).

Interestingly, the strongest arguments for a finding that these standards qualify as custom, at least as applied to the United States, are the same reasons why such a finding is likely moot; these standards related to law enforcement and the use of force by law enforcement appear to be wholly consistent with the laws of the United States, thus increasing the likelihood that they would be considered custom and therefore enforceable under international customary law (at least as applied to the United States), while at the same time removing the need for such enforcement internationally

(since domestic laws of the United States already

provide for such enforcement).

IN USING FATAL FORCE INCIDENT TO ARREST, IS IT POSSIBLE FOR AN OFFICER TO VIOLATE INTERNATIONAL LAW WITHOUT VIOLATING THE 4TH AMENDMENT?

Many of the binding international standards discussed earlier focus on subjective intent or state of mind of the officer who uses deadly force incident to arrest. Because the Supreme Court's Fourth Amendment analysis for fatal force incident to arrest is focused on what an objectively reasonable officer in the same circumstances would have done, there are may be instances where on officer's conduct in using deadly force incident to arrest would violate an international treaty, but would not violate Supreme Court's objective reasonableness test under the Fourth Amendment.

This may seem counter-intuitive, but there are situations in which fatal force by the officer conforms to the Fourth Amendment, and yet, still violates binding international law. However, as we will see, technical conformity to the Fourth Amendment in those situations may be irrelevant, since the conduct likely violates specific domestic criminal and civil standards.

We know from our analysis of the U.N. Convention Against Torture that if an officer shot and killed a suspect in order to punish the suspect for an act, or based on some discriminatory purpose, that shooting would violate the Convention. However, even assuming these facts to be true, if a reasonable officer (i.e. An officer who is not inclined to punish or discriminate) in that same position would have felt that the suspect posed a serious threat of immediate harm or death to another person or the officer, the officer's shooting of the suspect would not violate the Fourth Amendment, even though the officer actually acted with a subjective intent that is criminal (either to punish the suspect or based on discriminatory purpose).

The scenario outlined above with regard to racial discrimination would also violate Article 5(b) of the Convention on the Elimination of All Forms of Racial Discrimination, and yet, would not offend the Fourth Amendment.

Similarly, an officer who shoots and kills a suspect arbitrarily would be in violation of Article 6(1) of the International Covenant on Civil and Political Rights, but if a reasonable officer in that same position would have felt that the suspect posed a serious threat of immediate harm or death to another person or the officer, the officer's shooting of the suspect would not violate the Fourth Amendment. In this example, if we assume that facts do exist that would make a reasonable officer believe the suspect posed a serious threat of immediate death to the officer, but for whatever reason the actual officer is unaware of these facts (i.e. the actual officer is completely unreasonable, and is not concerned with the facts that would lead any other officer to believe that the suspect posed a serious risk of immediate death to the officer), but instead decides he will shoot and kill any person that he sees wearing a Yankees ballcap, his actions in shooting and killing the

Yankees fan are certainly arbitrary and violate Article 6(1), and yet, because the Supreme Court is concerned only with what a reasonable officer in the same situation would do, the conduct of the officer would not violate the Forth Amendment.

These apparent shortcomings of Fourth Amendment protections are possible only because the Supreme Court is not concerned with the actual underlying intent or motivation of the officer, and is only concerned with what a reasonable officer would do in that same situation. The Fourth Amendment is concerned with the objective, while most of the international treaties examined here are concerned with the subjective. The officer in the scenarios above violates international law because those laws are concerned with the officer's actual underlying intent or motivation. However, as previously mentioned, the fact that the racist, punitive, or arbitrary shooter technically has not violated the Fourth Amendment is likely irrelevant, since the shooter's actions in any of the three examples would violate a host of criminal and civil standards, and the shooter would likely be facing liability under those standards that would far exceed anything he might face for a Forth Amendment violation.

DEADLY FORCE BY GERMAN POLICE

While the legal analysis for use of force in the United States is largely a function of case law, the use of force analysis for German police is driven by statute. Since Germany is a civil law jurisdiction, as opposed to common law, the laws of Germany are driven primarily by statute, rather than case law (Exter & Kammer, 2001). The main sources of law in Germany are the constitution, statutes, executive orders, regulations, decrees, and charters (Exter & Kammer, 2001). In addition, German law is often influenced by the laws of the European Union, although domestic legislation is required for EU law to apply in Germany (Exter & Kammer, 2001).

German laws relevant to the use of force by officers will be analyzed, followed by a discussion of international standards that might also apply to fatal use of force by officers in Germany. Finally, German laws will be compared to applicable international standards to see if scenarios could exist in which an officer's actions would violate international standards without violating German law.

GERMAN LEGAL STANDARDS GOVERNING DEADLY FORCE

The Grundgesetz, GG (Basic Law for the Federal Republic of Germany, as amended 20 December 1993) is the Constitution for Germany. A number of provisions of the Grundgesetz appear to be relevant to issue of fatal use of force by officers incident to arrest, including Article 1 (dealing with human dignity), Article 2 (dealing with the right to life), Article 3 (equality before the law, regardless of race or origin), and Article 34 (dealing with liability of the government and agents) (Grundgesetz, 1993).

Article 1 states that "human dignity shall be inviolable. To respect and protect it shall be the duty of all state authority." (Grundgesetz, 1993, Art. 1, § 1).

Article 1 goes on to describe the basic rights outlined in

the constitution as "inviolable and inalienable" and

binding on the legislature, the executive, and the

judiciary "as directly applicable law" (Grundgesetz,

1993, Art. 1, §§ 2-3). Among these binding, inviolable,

inalienable, and directly applicable rights are the right

to life and the right to be equal before the law,

regardless of race (Grundgesetz, 1993, Art. 2, § 2; Art.

3, § 1 & 3). Article 34 describes liability for the

government and its agents as follows:

"If any person, in the exercise of a public office

entrusted to him, violates his official duty to a third

party, liability shall rest principally with the state or

public body that employs him. In the event of

intentional wrongdoing or gross negligence, the right of recourse against the individual officer shall be preserved. The ordinary courts shall not be closed to claims for compensation or indemnity."

(Grundgesetz, 1993, Art. 34).

On its face, the constitution seems to strictly prohibit both the taking of a human life and unequal treatment under the law based on race, and also seems to provide for personal liability where the government agent commits intentional wrongdoing or gross negligence. However, Article 2 does provide that the rights discussed in the constitution may be interfered with pursuant to a law (Grundgesetz, 1993, Art. 2, § 2).

A review of the Criminal Code, the Criminal Procedure Code, and the Code of Crimes Against International Law reveals no law that would permit unequal treatment under the law based on race. Thus, where it can be shown that an officer's use of fatal force is based on race, the officer's actions would violate the German Constitution. Even where there is no race-based unequal treatment, the officer's fatal use of force would still violate the constitutional prohibition on taking human life, unless the officer acted pursuant to a law. Here, we look to the German Criminal Code, the Criminal Procedure Code, and the Code of Crimes Against International Law to see if there is a law that would permit the taking of a life, and under what circumstances.

The Strafgesetzbuch, StGB (German Criminal Code) provides that a public official who commits bodily injury during the discharge of his duties may be held criminally liable (Strafgesetzbuch, § 340). The Criminal Code also provides that anyone who kills another without meeting the elements for murder will be punished for manslaughter (imprisonment of at least 5 years, but up to life for especially serious cases) (Strafgesetzbuch, § 212). The Criminal Code also provides for criminal liability for negligent homicide (Strafgesetzbuch, § 222). These sections of the Criminal Code seem to give specificity to the Constitutional right to life discussed earlier.

The Criminal Code also provides that an act that is done because it is required in order to avert imminent unlawful assault on a person (the actor or a third party) is not considered a criminal act (Strafgesetzbuch, § 32). The Code also provides that a person won't be punished even if they exceed the limits of the defense due to confusion, fear, or fright (Strafgesetzbuch, § 33). Section 34 of the Criminal Code provides for a kind of balancing test in necessity defenses:

"Whoever, faced with an imminent danger to life, limb, freedom, honor, property or another legal interest which cannot otherwise be averted, commits an act to avert the danger from himself or another, does not act unlawfully, if, upon weighing the conflicting interests, in particular the affected legal interests and the degree of danger threatening them, the protected interest substantially outweighs the one interfered with. This shall apply, however, only to the extent that the act is a proportionate means to avert the danger."

(Strafgesetzbuch, § 34).

In light of the necessity defense provided under the German Criminal Code, it appears that if an officer uses fatal force against a suspect incident to arrest, that officer's conduct violates both the criminal code and the constitution unless the officer's use of force is done either to avoid imminent unlawful assault, or the harm inflicted by the officer is proportionate to the danger faced, and in the totality of the circumstances, the legal interest that is being protected by the officer is substantially outweighed by the one interfered with.

Under the first necessity defense (imminent unlawful assault), an officer could use fatal force in Germany without violating the law as long as the fatal force was required in order to avoid imminent unlawful assault, and where the assault might not actually be imminent but the officer believes it to be based on fear, fright, or confusion, the officer's conduct will still be legal. Notice here that for the first necessity defense, there is no proportionality requirement; it doesn't really matter if the "imminent unlawful assault" threatened by the suspect is only a minor slap, even where the officer shoots and kills the suspect, so long as the shooting is required in order to avoid the unlawful assault.

To use an example that will come up again, if we assume that a suspect is committed to slapping another person in the face, and that such a slap would be unlawful, and further assume that the only way to keep the slap from occurring is to shoot the person, then an officer could shoot and kill the person without violating German law (since the first necessary defense would apply), notwithstanding the fact that the threatened harm is just a slap (albeit a violent and unlawful slap). This is true even where the belief in the necessity is due only to fear, confusion, or fright.

The second necessity defense that contemplates a balancing test may actually be a more difficult standard for the officer to meet, at least in the context of fatal use of force, because that defense requires a showing that "the protected interest substantially outweighs the one interfered with" (Strafgesetzbuch, §

34). Where the legal interest interfered with is the suspect's right to life, how can another interest substantially outweigh that interest? Even if the officer were protecting his own life--that is, the officer is actually facing death--can we say that the importance or value of the officer's life substantially outweighs the suspect's life? In any case, the first necessity defense seems more forgiving and would likely be the only applicable defense, at least in case where the officer's use of force is fatal.

The German Criminal Procedure Code (Strafprozeßordnung, StPO) is code is basically identical to the scope of U.S. Criminal procedure, so much of the substantive law here deals with issues that arise in court, long after the arrest. However, along the lines of the U.S. Supreme Court's discussion of fatal use of force as essentially a search and seizure issue, section 102 of the Criminal Procedure Code seems relevant to the topic, and reads in relevant part as follows:

"A body search, a search of the property and of the private and other premises of a person who, as a perpetrator or as an inciter or accessory before the fact, is suspected of committing a criminal offense, or is suspected of accessoryship after the fact or of obstruction of justice or of handling stolen goods, may be made for the purpose of his apprehension and in the cases where it may be presumed that the search will lead to the discovery of evidence."

(Strafprozeßordnung, StPO, § 102).

Although the Criminal Procedure Code is somewhat relevant to the issue of legality of seizures, it appears that the Criminal Code's description of homicide crimes and necessity defenses will control in questions of the legality of fatal force by officers. Similarly, additional sources of German law were reviewed, such as the Völkerstrafgesetzbuch (Act to Introduce the Code of Crimes Against International Law of 26 June 2002), but none of those laws provided any useful guidance on the specific issue of fatal use of force by domestic law enforcement officers incident to arrest (at least where the actions took place during peacetime and were not part of a broader plan that could amount to genocide).

GERMAN POLICE DEPARTMENT POLICIES ON DEADLY FORCE

The structure of German Police Departments is federal in nature, with few uniform national standards (Frevel & Kuschewski, 2009). With 16 different states in Germany, and some parallel or overlapping jurisdictions, this means that there are potentially 16 or more distinct policies on the use of deadly force throughout Germany (Frevel & Kuschewski, 2009). Although there is some uniformity at the academy training level for cadets to use firearms only as a last resort, each state in Germany can develop its own written departmental policies on the use of deadly force (Frevel & Kuschewski, 2009; Stute, 2014).

Thus, the only real restrictions keeping vastly divergent deadly force policies from developing throughout Germany are the broad legal parameters discussed above, and the substantial training and indoctrination for new officers that teaches officers to use deadly force only as a last resort. Even given the possibility of divergent policies, it follows that the content of each policy will, at a minimum, be consistent with the laws discussed above (i.e. Officers use force only to avoid imminent harm), even if the form of each policy differs.

RATES OF GERMAN POLICE USE OF DEADLY FORCE

Unlike in the United States, Germany seems to lack publicly-accessible statistics on fatal use of force by officers (Amnesty International, 2004). Despite this lack of consistent data, some figures on use of force and firearms by German police are publicly accessible. For example, there were eight fatalities due to interactions with German police from 2012 to 2014, and 109 deaths by service weapons in Germany from 1998-2014 (Stute, 2014).

During the year 2011, German police officers fired a total of only 85 bullets (NBC.com, 2012). Of those 85 shots fired, 49 were warning shots (NBC.com,

2012). In total, six people were killed by German police in 2011, down from seven killed by German police in 2010 (NBC.com, 2012). In contrast, there were over 700 arrest-related deaths in the United States in 2009 (Burch, 2011).

Some commentators have noted that some the differences in fatal use of force between Germany and the U.S. may be due to the fact that German officers are much less likely to encounter armed suspects than their American counterparts are, and due to the fact that German officers spend nearly three years in training that emphasizes using firearms only as a last resort (Stute, 2014).

APPLICABLE INTERNATIONAL STANDARDS THAT COULD GOVERN DEADLY FORCE IN GERMANY

Germany is party to the three applicable treaties discussed under binding international law in the U.S. (University of Minnesota, 2015). As previously discussed, it appears that UN Convention against Torture and Other Cruel, Inhuman or Degrading Treatment or Punishment could be applicable to some cases of fatal use of force, at least where it can be shown that the officer committed the act for a discriminatory purpose or to punish the suspect for an act. Similarly, International Covenant on Civil and Political Rights is violated where the officer uses fatal force to deprive a suspect of life arbitrarily (Article 6) or where the officer uses fatal force with discriminatory intent (Article 26). Finally, the International Convention on the Elimination of all Forms of Racial Discrimination is violated where the officer inflicts violence or death on an individual due to race or a race-related characteristic.

In addition to the treaties previously discussed (that are binding on both the U.S. and Germany), there are a number of treaties that Germany is bound to (but not the U.S.), including the European Convention for the Protection of Human Rights and Fundamental Freedoms, and the European Convention for the Prevention of Torture and Inhuman or Degrading Treatment or Punishment. However, European Convention for the Prevention of Torture and Inhuman or Degrading Treatment or Punishment (ECPT), as well as the two protocols thereto, only establishes a committee; the ECPT does not specify any substantive enforceable rights or protections, aside from administrative procedures concerning the creation and maintenance of the committee (European Convention for the Prevention of Torture and Inhuman or Degrading Treatment or Punishment, 1987).

European Convention for the Protection of Human Rights and Fundamental Freedoms

Germany signed the European Convention for the Protection of Human Rights and Fundamental Freedoms (ECHR) on November 4, 1950, ratified the ECHR on December 5, 1952, and the ECHR entered into force on September 3, 1953 (University of Minnesota, 2015). Germany also ratified a number of protocols to the treaty, but only Article 2 of the ECHR is relevant to the use of deadly force by officers incident to arrest.

Article 2 of the ECHR reads as follows:

"Everyone's right to life shall be protected by law... Deprivation of life shall not be regarded as inflicted in contravention of this article when it results from the use of force which is no more than absolutely necessary:
a) in defense of any person from unlawful violence;
b) in order to effect a lawful arrest or to prevent the escape of a person lawfully detained;

c) in action lawfully taken for the purpose of quelling a riot or insurrection."

(Art. 2, European Convention for the Protection of Human Rights and Fundamental Freedoms, 1950).

The use of fatal force by an officer incident to arrest would violate the European Convention for the Protection of Human Rights and Fundamental Freedoms, unless the officer uses no more force than absolutely necessary, in defense of any person from unlawful violence, or in order to effect lawful arrest or prevent lawfully detained person from escaping. Notice under this legal standard there is no requirement of proportionality, nor is there any explicit weighing of the harm inflicted against the harm avoided. It is true that the force must be "no more force than absolutely necessary," but the harm being avoided does not have to be life-threatening.

Under the unlawful violence prong, there is no requirement for the person being threatened with violence to be threatened with fatal violence, only that the shooting is absolutely necessary to stop the unlawful violence. So, if we assume that a suspect is committed to slapping another person in the face, and that such a slap would be unlawful, and further assume that the only way to keep the slap from occurring is to shoot the person (the officer is too far away to stop the slap by any other means, and the victim is incapacitated or otherwise unable to stop the slap), then an officer could shoot and kill the person without violating the

ECHR, notwithstanding the fact that the threatened harm is just a slap (albeit a violent and unlawful slap).

As absurd as that fact scenario is, the 'lawful arrest' and 'lawful detention' test is open to an even more offensive result. Since the lawful arrest and lawful detention has no proportionality requirement, and since there isn't even a threat of unlawful violence requirement here, a person who is resisting arrest for ANY offense can be shot and killed, even if the person isn't using violence or the threat of violence to resist, so long as the force used is no more than absolutely necessary to effect the arrest or prevent the escape.

For example, if we assume that someone guilty of the lowest level of offense for which a person can be arrested in Germany (perhaps petty theft or possession of a small amount of a controlled substance), and we assume that the officer encounters the suspect (who he cannot identify by name) in a field while the officer is on foot, and we assume that the suspect happens to be the fastest runner on earth, and further assume that when the suspect runs from the officer, the only means available to the officer to effect an arrest or prevent escape is to shoot the suspect in the back, the officer could shoot and kill the suspect here without violating the European Convention for the Protection of Human Rights and Fundamental Freedoms. This is true even though the crime was a minor offense, with no violence or threat of violence to the officer or any other person.

IN USING FATAL FORCE INCIDENT TO ARREST,
IS IT POSSIBLE FOR AN OFFICER TO VIOLATE
INTERNATIONAL LAW WITHOUT VIOLATING
GERMAN LAW?

The analysis here is somewhat tortured, as it should be; domestic law in Germany is generally consistent with binding international law, so we would expect that a violation of one would necessarily mean a violation of the other. The question itself cannot be approached in the same manner that it is presented, since we are really looking for the exceptional case, not the normal fact pattern. Instead of looking first at those acts that violate international law, and then looking to see if any of those same acts would be legal under German law, it might make sense to first look at the easiest possible method of qualifying for a necessity defense under German law (this assumes that the conduct is otherwise illegal under German law), and then examine whether any of the binding international treaties could still be violated by the same conduct that is legal under domestic German law (due to the application of the necessity defense).

Our analysis of necessity defenses under German law revealed two types of necessity defenses, one that required only a belief in the necessity of force in order to avoid imminent unlawful assault, even if that belief is based on fear, confusion, or fright (the first necessity defense), and a second necessity defense that contemplated a balancing test, with no "fear, confusion, or fright" exception.

The second necessity defense contemplates a balancing test that probably could not be met without also making the act legal under international law. However, as previously discussed, the first necessity defense has no similar proportionality test.

In theory, an officer who shoots and kills a suspect incident to arrest could violate applicable international law and still qualify for a necessity defense under German law, at least under the first necessity defense discussed, which only requires that fatal force be used to avoid imminent unlawful assault, or that the officer at least believe this to be true (based on fear, fright, or confusion).

Recall the hypothetical discussed earlier, in which the fearful, frightened, or confused officer believed that shooting a suspect was the only way to prevent a suspect from unlawfully slapping another person? In that hypothetical, the officer's conduct did not violate German law, since he qualified for the necessity defense. If we were to assume further that the officer's fear, fright, or confusion was due to a race-based discriminatory belief, it would appear that the officer's conduct would violate international law (the International Convention on the Elimination of all Forms of Racial Discrimination) and yet, still not violate domestic German law.

IN USING FATAL FORCE INCIDENT TO ARREST,
IS IT POSSIBLE FOR AN OFFICER TO VIOLATE
GERMAN LAW WITHOUT VIOLATING THE 4TH
AMENDMENT OF THE U.S. CONSTITUTION?

Similar to the approach used in the international vs. German law analysis, it may be most efficient to first examine what types of egregious use of fatal force by law enforcement would survive Fourth Amendment scrutiny, and then explore whether those facts could nonetheless be made to not qualify for a necessity defense under German law.

As has been suggested in earlier Fourth Amendment analysis, the easiest point to exploit in the Fourth Amendment analysis as applied to fatal use of force incident to arrest is the fact that the Supreme Court is wholly unconcerned with the officer's actual subjective intent or state of mind. The Court is only concerned with what a reasonable officer would do in the same situation, based on the totality of the circumstances. So, if there is a way to avoid application of the necessity defense based solely on the officer's subjective intent or state of mind, then there may be a way to violate German law without offending the Fourth Amendment of the U.S.Constitution.

That second necessity defense contemplates the same kind of objective balancing that the Supreme Court uses in its Fourth Amendment analysis. It seems unlikely that a given hypothetical would survive the Fourth Amendment but fail the balancing test from the second necessity defense. However, the first necessity defense seems to only be focused on subjective intent or state of mind of the officer, so it is possible that a hypothetical could pass the Fourth Amendment analysis (objectively reasonable) and still fail the first necessity defense.

First, assume an officer is in a position in which a reasonable officer would believe, based on the totality of the circumstances, that the suspect poses a serious threat of imminent harm or death to the officer. Further assume that this particular officer who shoots and kills the suspect does not actually believe that the shooting is necessary to avoid imminent unlawful assault (i.e. the officer is unreasonable) but that the officer actually shoots the suspect for some other reason. Under this hypothetical, the officer's actions would not violate the Fourth Amendment, and would seem to violate German law, as the first necessity defense would not apply.

The second part of the analysis is to see if there is a way to prevent that second necessity defense (that resembles the Fourth Amendment) from applying, without causing the hypothetical to violate the Fourth Amendment. The hypothetical will fail the second necessity defense where the protected interest (the officer's life) does not substantially outweigh the life of the suspect.

Thus, it appears that under this very specific and tortured hypothetical involving the ignorant, unreasonable, murderous officer, who stumbles into a deadly situation without realizing it, the officer's use of

deadly force incident to arrest would violate German

law without violating the Fourth Amendment of the

U.S. Constitution.

CONCLUSION

U.S. law on the use of fatal force by officers is generally consistent with the spirit of both international law and German law on the subject. In fact, it is surprising how similar U.S. and German law are, especially considering the historical and political differences between the two nations. Similarly, even though officers in Germany are much less likely to face armed suspects than their American counterparts are, the laws regarding the use of force in both countries are remarkably similar.

Yet despite the many similarities among U.S. Law, International law, and German law, it is indeed possible for an officer's use of fatal force incident to arrest to violate German law without violating the Fourth Amendment, just as it is possible to violate International law without violating German law, or to violate International law without violating the Fourth Amendment.

REFERENCES

Amnesty International (2004). Back in the spotlight : allegations of police ill-treatment and excessive use of force in Germany.

BAJI (2014). BAJI 3.43: Care Required by Law Enforcement Officers in Using Deadly Force-Prior Tactical Conduct and Decisions. Spring 2014.

Brown, E. (2014). Timeline:Michael Brown Shooting in Ferguson, Mo. USA Today. December 2, 2014. Available online at: http://www.usatoday.com/story/news/nation/2014/08/14/michael-brown-ferguson-missouri-timeline/14051827/ (Accessed April 28, 2015).

Burch, A.M. (2011). Arrest-Related Deaths, 2003-2009 Statistical Tables. U.S. Department of Justice, Bureau of Justice Statistics.November, 2011. Available online at: http://www.bjs.gov/content/pub/pdf/ard0309st.pdf (Accessed April 28, 2015).

California Penal Code § 835a.

CBS News (2015). DOJ Clears Darren Wilson in Michael Brown Killing. CBS News. March 4, 2015. Available online at: http://www.cbsnews.com/news/darren-wilson-cleared-in-michael-brown-ferguson-killing-by-justice-department/ (Accessed April 28, 2015).

Chuck, E. (2014). The Killing of an Unarmed Teen:
What We Know About Brown's Death. NBC News.
August 13, 2014. Available online at:
http://www.nbcnews.com/storyline/michael-brown-
shooting/killing-unarmed-teen-what-we-know-about-
browns-death-n178696 (Accessed April 28, 2015).

CIA (2015a). The World Factbook: United States.
Central Intelligence Agency. Available online at:
https://www.cia.gov/library/publications/the-world-
factbook/geos/us.html (Accessed April 1, 2015).

CIA (2015b). The World Factbook: Germany. Central
Intelligence Agency. Available online at:
https://www.cia.gov/library/publications/the-world-
factbook/geos/gm.html (Accessed April 1, 2015).

Council of Europe, European Convention for the Prevention of Torture and Inhuman or Degrading Treatment or Punishment, 26 November 1987, ETS 126, available at: http://www.refworld.org/docid/3ae6b36314.html [accessed 8 May 2015]

Council of Europe, European Convention for the Protection of Human Rights and Fundamental Freedoms, as amended by Protocols Nos. 11 and 14, 4 November 1950, ETS 5, available at: http://www.refworld.org/docid/3ae6b3b04.html [accessed 30 April 2015]

Exter, R. & Kammer, M. (2001). Legal Research in

Germany at the Crossroads of Traditional and

Electronic Media: An Overview. Law and Technology

Resources for Legal Professionals. Available online at:

http://www.llrx.com/features/germanlaw.htm (Accessed

April 28, 2015).

Frevel, B. & Kuschewski,P. (2009). Police

Organization and Police Reform in Germany:The Case

of North Rhine-Westphalia. German Police Studies,

Vol. 5, No. 2. 49-89.

Gallagher, A. T. (2010). The International Law of

Human Trafficking. New York: Cambridge University

Press.

Graham v. Connor (1989) 490 U.S. 386.

Grundgesetz, GG (Basic Law for the Federal Republic

of Germany, as amended 20 December 1993).

Available online at:

http://www.iuscomp.org/gla/statutes/GG.htm (Accessed

April 4th, 2015).

Hernandez v. City of Pomona (2009) 46 Cal. 4th 501.

Leonnig, C. D. (2014). Current Law Gives Police Wide

Latitude to Use Deadly Force: Ferguson Shooting Case

Renews Debate Over Whether Officers Have too Much

Leeway, too Little Accountability. Washington Post.

August 28, 2014. Available online at:

http://www.washingtonpost.com/politics/current-law-gives-police-wide-latitude-to-use-deadly-

force/2014/08/28/768090c4-2d64-11e4-994d-

202962a9150c_story.html (Accessed April 1, 2014).

McElvain, J. P. (2009). Police Shootings and Citizen

Behavior. El Paso, TX: LFB Scholarly Publications.

NBC.com (2012). German Police Fired Just 85 Bullets

Total in 2011. NBC News. May 11, 2012. Available

online at:

http://worldnews.nbcnews.com/_news/2012/05/11/1166

2345-german-police-fired-just-85-bullets-total-in-2011

(Accessed April 29, 2015).

 Organization of American States (2015). American

Convention on Human Rights, General Information of

the Treaty: B-32. OAS, Department of International
Law. Available online at:
http://www.oas.org/dil/treaties_B-
32_American_Convention_on_Human_Rights_sign.ht
m (Accessed April 29, 2015).

Perez-Pena, R. (2015). Fatal Police Shootings:
Accounts Since Ferguson. New York Times. April 8,
2015. Available online at:
http://www.nytimes.com/interactive/2015/04/08/us/fatal
-police-shooting-accounts.html?_r=0 (Accessed April
28, 2015).

Strafprozeßordnung, StPO (Criminal Procedure Code).
Available online at:

http://www.iuscomp.org/gla/statutes/StPO.htm

(Accessed April 4th, 2015).

Strafgesetzbuch, StGB (Criminal Code). Available

online at:

http://www.iuscomp.org/gla/statutes/StGB.htm

(Accessed April 4th, 2015).

Stute, D. (2014). Why German Police Officers Rarely

Reach for Their Guns. Deutsche Welle news. August

27, 2014. Available online at:

http://www.dw.de/why-german-police-officers-

rarely-reach-for-their-guns/a-17884779 (Accessed

April 4th, 2015).

Tennessee v. Garner (1985) 471 U.S. 1.

Title 42, United States Code § 1983.

University of Minnesota (2015). Ratification of
International Human Rights Treaties--Germany.
University of Minnesota: Human Rights Library.
Available online at:
https://www1.umn.edu/humanrts/research/ratification-
germany.html (Accessed April 29, 2015).

U.N. Convention Against Torture and Other Cruel,
Inhuman or Degrading Treatment or Punishment, G.A.
Res. 39/46, U.N. GAOR, 39th Sess., Annex, Agenda
Item 99, U.N. Doc. No. A/RES/39/708 (1984),
reprinted in 23 I.L.M. 1027 (1984), as modified 24
I.L.M. 535 (1985).

UN General Assembly, International Covenant on Civil and Political Rights, 16 December 1966, United Nations, Treaty Series, vol. 999, p. 171, available at: http://www.refworld.org/docid/3ae6b3aa0.html [accessed 30 April 2015]

UN General Assembly, International Convention on the Elimination of All Forms of Racial Discrimination, 21 December 1965, United Nations, Treaty Series, vol. 660, p. 195, available at: http://www.refworld.org/docid/3ae6b3940.html [accessed 30 April 2015]

UN General Assembly, Universal Declaration of Human Rights, 10 December 1948, 217 A (III), available at:

http://www.refworld.org/docid/3ae6b3712c.html

[accessed 30 April 2015]

UN General Assembly, Code of conduct for law enforcement officials, 5 February 1980, A/RES/34/169 , available at:

http://www.refworld.org/docid/48abd572e.html

[accessed 30 April 2015]

UN General Assembly, Basic Principles on the Use of Force and Firearms by Law Enforcement Officials, 18 December 1990, 45/121.

About the author

Michael Caves has taught and designed graduate and undergraduate courses at universities throughout the United States in various subjects, including criminal investigation, ethics, organizational behavior, and legal studies. Michael has a Bachelor's degree in communications, a Master's degree in conflict resolution, a Master's degree in Public Administration, a Doctorate in jurisprudence, a Masters of Laws (LL.M.) in international criminal law and justice, and a Ph.D. in rhetoric and communication. Michael has been a criminal prosecutor in the United States since 2007.